KNIGHT

Angels hm

CAROLS
FOR CHOIRS
2

FIFTY CAROLS FOR
CHRISTMAS AND ADVENT

Edited and arranged by

DAVID WILLCOCKS
AND
JOHN RUTTER

MUSIC DEPARTMENT

OXFORD UNIVERSITY PRESS

WALTON STREET   200 MADISON AVENUE
OXFORD, OX2 6DP   NEW YORK, N.Y. 10016

4-50

Oxford University Press, Walton Street, Oxford OX2 6DP

London New York Toronto
Delhi Bombay Calcutta Madras Karachi
Kuala Lumpur Singapore Hong Kong Tokyo
Nairobi Dar es Salaam Cape Town
Melbourne Auckland
and associated companies in
Beirut Berlin Ibadan Mexico City Nicosia

© *Oxford University Press 1970*

*All rights reserved. No part of this publication may be
reproduced, performed, stored in a retrieval system, or
transmitted, in any form or by any means, electronic,
mechanical, photocopying, recording, or otherwise, without
the prior permission of Oxford University Press or the
appropriate licensing authority*

*This book is sold subject to the condition that it shall not, by
way of trade or otherwise, be lent, re-sold, hired out, or
otherwise circulated without the publisher's prior consent in
any form of binding or cover other than that in which it is
published and without a similar condition including this
condition being imposed on the subsequent purchaser*

ISBN 0-19-353565-3

Details of orchestrations for carols in the collections *Carols for Choirs
1, 2,* and *3,* are given in the *Oxford Music for Christmas* catalogue. The
carols in this book, for which orchestral accompaniments are available on
hire, are indicated by † in the Index of Titles and First Lines overleaf.

The gramophone record *Carols for Choirs* (OUP 150) contains 14
titles selected from the three collections, performed by the Bach Choir
with the Philip Jones Brass Ensemble, conducted by David Willcocks.

*Printed in Great Britain
at the University Press, Oxford
by David Stanford
Printer to the University*

PREFACE

Carols for Choirs 2 has been compiled as a companion volume to *Carols for Choirs 1* to meet the needs of choirs and choral societies wishing to perform complete services or concerts of carols without the inconvenience of handling a number of separate leaflets and books. A further fifty carols have been selected, many of them from traditional sources and newly arranged by the present Editors or in settings by other distinguished musicians past and present. Among the original compositions included are carols by Benjamin Britten, Richard Rodney Bennett, William Mathias and William Walton.

The ten years which have elapsed since the appearance of *Carols for Choirs 1* have seen a steady growth in the number of carol concerts given by choral societies, often with orchestral accompaniment. With the needs of these occasions in mind, the Editors have included a number of secular carols and also a generous proportion of carols which may be orchestrally accompanied if desired. Most of these accompaniments call for no more than modest orchestral resources, and many of them may be performed by strings alone; parts are available on hire.

Advent Carol Services have also grown in popularity, notably in schools and colleges where it is not possible to celebrate Christmas during term-time, but no generally accepted form of service has hitherto existed. The Revd. David Edwards, sometime Dean of King's College, Cambridge, has drawn up for this book an Order of Service based on the annual Advent Carol Service held in King's College Chapel, and has written a Bidding Prayer; the Matin Responsory (with which the service opens) and a number of carols suitable for Advent have also been included. Provision has thus been made for the needs of a complete Advent Carol Service.

Care has been taken to ensure that most of the carols included in the book lie within the capacity of the average choir and that as many styles and periods as possible are represented.

Note

O come, all ye faithful and *Hark! the herald angels sing* have been included in an appendix. Extended versions of these two hymns are contained in *Carols for Choirs 1*.

INDEX OF TITLES AND FIRST LINES

Where first lines differ from titles the former are shown in italics.

Carols suitable for unaccompanied singing are marked thus*.
Carols with orchestral material available on hire are marked thus†.

CAROL	COMPOSER/ARRANGER	NO.	PAGE
*A BABE IS BORN I WYS	F. Bainton	*1*	6
†*A CHILD IS BORN IN BETHLEHEM	Scheidt ed. David Willcocks	*2*	7
A NEW YEAR CAROL	Benjamin Britten	*13*	64
*ADAM LAY YBOUNDEN	Boris Ord	*3*	10
*ALL MY HEART THIS NIGHT REJOICES	J. G. Ebeling	*4*	12
*ALL THIS TIME	William Walton	*5*	13
†*ANGELS AND THE SHEPHERDS, THE	Bohemian trad. arr. C. H. Trevor	*39*	182
†*Born in a stable so bare*	John Rutter	*6*	16
†*CHERRY TREE CAROL, THE	English trad. arr. David Willcocks	*22*	92
†COME LEAVE YOUR SHEEP	French trad. arr. John Rutter	*37*	169
†COME, THOU REDEEMER OF THE EARTH	German trad. arr. David Willcocks	*16*	71
*DECK THE HALL	Welsh trad. arr. David Willcocks	*7*	22
†DING DONG! MERRILY ON HIGH	16th cent. French arr. David Willcocks	*8*	28
†DOWN IN YON FOREST	English trad. arr. John Rutter	*9*	32
†*GABRIEL'S MESSAGE	Basque Noël arr. David Willcocks	*43*	191
*†*Gloria sei dir gesungen*	J. S. Bach ed. John Rutter	*50A*	219
*†*Glory now to God we render*	J. S. Bach ed. John Rutter	*50A*	219
†*Going through the hills*	John Rutter	*10*	39
*HAIL! BLESSED VIRGIN MARY	Italian carol arr. Charles Wood	*11*	50
†HARK! THE HERALD ANGELS SING	adapted from Mendelssohn	*App. 1*	221
†HE IS BORN THE DIVINE CHRIST CHILD	French trad. arr. John Rutter	*17*	74
Here we bring new water	Benjamin Britten	*13*	64
†HERE WE COME A-WASSAILING	English trad. arr. John Rutter	*12*	51
*HOLLY AND THE IVY, THE	English trad. arr. Walford Davies	*44*	196
†HOW FAR IS IT TO BETHLEHEM?	English trad. arr. David Willcocks	*14*	66
I look from afar	Adapted from Palestrina	*15*	68
†*I saw a fair maiden*	R. R. Terry	*19*	84
*I SAW A MAIDEN	Basque Noël arr. E. Pettman	*18*	83
†I SING OF A MAIDEN	Patrick Hadley	*20*	86
†IL EST NÉ LE DIVIN ENFANT	French trad. arr. John Rutter	*17*	74
†*INFANT KING, THE	Basque Noël arr. David Willcocks	*41*	188
†IT CAME UPON THE MIDNIGHT CLEAR	English trad. adapted Sullivan arr. David Willcocks	*21*	89
†*Joseph was an old man*	English trad. arr. David Willcocks	*22*	92
†LORD AT FIRST DID ADAM MAKE, THE	English trad. arr. David Willcocks	*45*	198
†MASTERS IN THIS HALL	French trad. arr. David Willcocks	*23*	94
*MATIN RESPONSORY	adapted from Palestrina	*15*	68
†MYN LYKING	R. R. Terry	*19*	84
†NATIVITY CAROL	John Rutter	*6*	16
NEW YEAR CAROL, A	Benjamin Britten	*13*	64
†NOËL NOUVELET	French trad. arr. John Rutter	*24*	100
†*Now the holly bears a berry*	English trad. arr. John Rutter	*25*	107
†*Nowell, nowell*	William Mathias	*26*	114

CAROL	COMPOSER/ARRANGER	NO.	PAGE
†NOWELL, SING NOWELL	French trad. arr. John Rutter	24	100
†O COME, ALL YE FAITHFUL	J. F. Wade	App. 2	222
†O COME, O COME, EMMANUEL	15th cent. French Processional arr. David Willcocks	27	120
*O sleep thou heav'n-born treasure	Leuner arr. Macpherson	28	123
†OF THE FATHER'S HEART BEGOTTEN	from Piae Cantiones; arr. David Willcocks	29	128
†On the first day of Christmas	English trad. arr. John Rutter	30	134
†ONCE IN ROYAL DAVID'S CITY	H. J. Gauntlett harm. A. H. Mann arr. David Willcocks	31	148
*OUT OF YOUR SLEEP	Richard Rodney Bennett	32	150
†PAST THREE A CLOCK	English trad. arr. John Rutter	33	153
†PATAPAN	Burgundian arr. Reginald Jacques	49	212
†PERSONENT HODIE	German, 1360, arr. Gustav Holst	34	160
†QUELLE EST CETTE ODEUR AGRÉABLE?	French trad. arr. David Willcocks	35	162
*QUEM PASTORES LAUDAVERE	14th cent. German arr. John Rutter	36	166
†QUITTEZ, PASTEURS	French trad. arr. John Rutter	37	169
†RESONEMUS LAUDIBUS	14th cent. arr. David Willcocks	38	177
†SANS DAY CAROL, THE	English trad. arr. John Rutter	25	107
*SHEPHERDS' CRADLE SONG, THE	Leuner arr. Macpherson	28	123
*SHEPHERDS LEFT THEIR FLOCKS A-STRAYING	14th cent. German arr. John Rutter	36	166
†*Shepherds, O hark ye	Bohemian trad. arr. C. H. Trevor	39	182
†SHEPHERD'S PIPE CAROL	John Rutter	10	39
†*SILENT NIGHT	Gruber arr. David Willcocks	40	184
†*Sing lullaby!	Basque Noël arr. David Willcocks	41	188
†SIR CHRISTÈMAS	William Mathias	26	114
†*The angel Gabriel from heaven came	Basque Noël arr. David Willcocks	43	191
*THERE IS NO ROSE	15th cent. English ed. John Stevens	42	190
*This is the truth sent from above	English trad. arr. R. Vaughan Williams	46	202
*TOMORROW SHALL BE MY DANCING DAY	English trad. arr. David Willcocks	47	203
*TRUTH FROM ABOVE, THE	English trad. arr. R. Vaughan Williams	46	202
†TWELVE DAYS OF CHRISTMAS, THE	English trad. arr. John Rutter	30	134
†WHENCE IS THAT GOODLY FRAGRANCE FLOWING?	French trad. arr. David Willcocks	35	162
†WHILE SHEPHERDS WATCHED THEIR FLOCKS	from Este's Psalter; arr. David Willcocks	48	210
† Willie, take your little drum	Burgundian arr. Reginald Jacques	49	212
†ZION HEARS THE WATCHMEN'S VOICES	J. S. Bach ed. John Rutter	50	214
†ZION HÖRT DIE WÄCHTER SINGEN	J. S. Bach ed. John Rutter	50	214
AN ADVENT CAROL SERVICE			223

1. A BABE IS BORN I WYS

F. BAINTON

2. On Christmas Day at morn,
This little child was born
To save us all that were forlorn,
And Jesus is his name.

3. On Good Friday so soon
To death he was all done,
Betwixt the time of morn and noon,
And Jesus is his name.

4. On Easter Day so swythe
He rose from death to life
To make us all both glad and blythe,
And Jesus is his name.

5. And on Ascension Day
To heav'n he took his way,
There to abide for aye and aye,
And Jesus is his name.

The words, taken from an old MS. in Westminster Abbey Library, have been slightly modernised.
Wys = know of a certainty.   *Swythe* = quickly, instantly.
Reprinted from the *University Carol Book* by permission of H. Freeman & Co.

2. A CHILD IS BORN IN BETHLEHEM

(Puer natus in Bethlehem)

Vv. 1 and 2 DAVID WILLCOCKS
(V. 1 translated from the Latin)
Vv. 3 and 4 from *The Cowley Carol Book*

SAMUEL SCHEIDT (1587–1654)
edited by DAVID WILLCOCKS

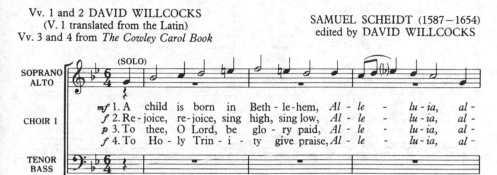

If preferred the piece may be sung a tone higher.
Also available separately (X144)
Verses 3 and 4 reprinted by permission of A. R. Mowbray & Co., Ltd.
Source: *Cantiones Sacrae Octo Vocum*, 1620

© Oxford University Press 1966

*(orig. ♩ in all voices)

3. ADAM LAY YBOUNDEN

Words anon. 15th century

BORIS ORD

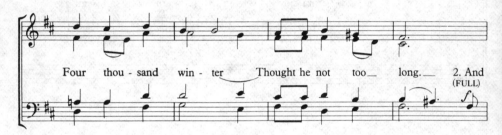

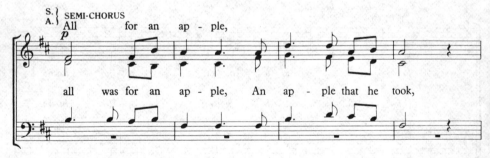

Reprinted by permission of Novello & Co., Ltd.

© Novello & Co. Ltd. 1957

3. Ne had the ap-ple tak-en been, The ap-ple tak-en been, __

Ne had nev-er our __ la - dy A - been hea-ven-é __ queen.

4. Bless - ed be the time That ap - ple tak-en was,

There - fore we moun sing - en, De-o gra - - - ci - as, De - o

gra - - - - - - ci -

- as, De - o gra - - - - - ci - as!

gra - - ci - as, __ De - o gra - - ci - as!

- as, De - o gra - - - - - - ci - as!

4. ALL MY HEART THIS NIGHT REJOICES

Words by PAULUS GERHARDT (1606—76)
tr. CATHERINE WINKWORTH

JOHANN GEORG EBELING
(1637?—76)

1. All my heart this night re-joi - ces
2. Hark! a voice from yon-der man - ger,
3. Come, then, let us has-ten yon - der!
4. Thee, dear Lord, with heed I'll che - rish,

As I hear, Far and near, Sweet-est an-gel voi - ces;
Soft and sweet, Doth en-treat, 'Flee from woe and dan - ger!
Here let all, Great and small, Kneel in awe and won - der!
Live to thee, And with thee, Dy-ing, shall not per - ish;

'Christ is born,' their choirs are sing - ing,
Breth-ren, come! from all doth grieve you,
Love him who with love is yearn - ing!
But shall dwell with thee for ev - er,

Till the air Ev-'ry-where Now with joy is ring - ing.
You are freed; All you need I will sure-ly give you.'
Hail the star That from far Bright with hope is burn - ing!
Far on high, In the joy That can al-ter nev - er.

5. ALL THIS TIME

Words 16th century

WILLIAM WALTON

All this time this song is best: 'Ver-bum ca - ro fac-tum est.'

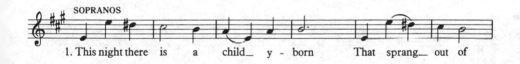

1. This night there is a child— y - born That sprang— out of

Jes - se's— thorn; We must— sing and say— there - forn,

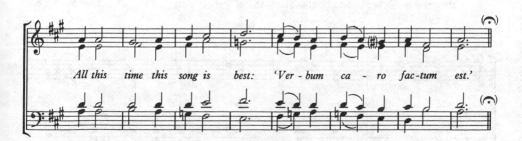

All this time this song is best: 'Ver - bum ca - ro fac-tum est.'

Words from *The Early English Carols* ed. R. L. Greene (Clarendon Press)

Also available separately (X201)

© Oxford University Press 1970

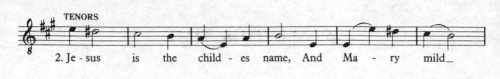

TENORS

2. Je - sus   is   the   child - es   name, And   Ma - ry   mild_

is_   his   dame;   All_   our   sor-row shall   turn_   to   game:

All   this   time   this   song   is   best: 'Ver - bum   ca - ro

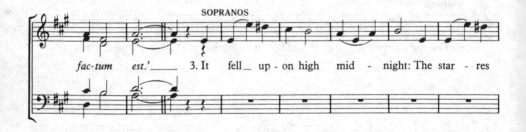

SOPRANOS

fac-tum   est.'_   3. It   fell_   up - on high   mid - night: The   star - res

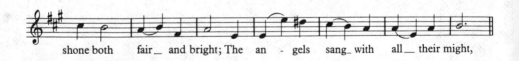

shone both   fair_ and bright; The   an - gels   sang_ with   all_   their might,

All   this   time   this   song   is   best: 'Ver - bum   ca - ro

fac - tum est.'_____ 4. Now kneel we down on our knee, And

pray we to the Tri - ni - ty Our help, our suc - cour

for to be; *All this time this song is best:* 'Ver - bum

mf cresc. **rit.**

ca - ro fac - tum est; Ver - bum ca - ro, Ver - bum

mf cresc.

ff

ca - ro, Ver - bum ca - ro fac - tum___ est.'_____

ff

6. NATIVITY CAROL

Words and music by
JOHN RUTTER

Also available separately (X169)

© Oxford University Press 1967

star____ He____ who loved____ us so.____   Far__ a - way____
rare,____ Hearts with his warmth he fills.____

si - lent he lay,____   sempre cresc.

si - lent lay, ____   Born__ to - day,__ your hom - age

si - lent he lay,____

si - lent lay,____   sempre cresc.

(omit small notes on piano)

7. DECK THE HALL

Words traditional

Welsh traditional carol
arranged by DAVID WILLCOCKS

Also available separately (X200)

© Oxford University Press 1970

★ Pronounce 'har' as 'ar' in *barrel*.

Cadenza ad lib.†, tempo rubato

molto rit.   **Presto**

★ Bracketed notes are optional.

† Conductors should feel free to omit the cadenza, or to substitute their own.

8. DING DONG! MERRILY ON HIGH

Words by
G. R. WOODWARD

16th cent. French tune
arranged by DAVID WILLCOCKS

1. Ding dong! mer-ri-ly on high in heav'n the bells are ring - ing: Ding dong! ve-ri-ly the sky is riv'n with an - gel sing - ing.
2. E'en so here be-low, be - low, let stee - ple bells be swung - en, And i - o, i -o, i -o, by priest and peo - ple sung - en.

Melody and words reprinted from *The Cambridge Carol Book* by permission
Also available separately (X196)

© Oxford University Press 1970

- ri - a, Ho - san - na in ex - cel - sis!

- ri - a,_ Ho - san - na in ex - cel - sis!

- ri - a, Ho - san - na_ in ex - cel - sis!

- ri - a, Ho - san - na in ex - cel - sis!

SOPRANOS (and ALTOS)

3. Pray you, du-ti-ful-ly prime   your

ma - tin chime, ye ring - ers;

TENORS and BASSES

May you beau-ti-ful-ly

rime   your eve-time song, ye sing - ers.

for E. T. C.

9. DOWN IN YON FOREST

English traditional carol
arranged by JOHN RUTTER

Melody and words reprinted by permission of Stainer & Bell, Ltd.
Arrangement from *Eight Christmas Carols* (Set 2)

© Oxford University Press 1967

love my Lord Je - sus a - bove a - ny - thing.___

SOPRANO
ALTO

*Ah*___

TENOR
BASS

A

2. In___ that hall___ there stands___ a bed: *The bells of pa - ra - dise*

*The bells*___

*Ah*___   *Ah*___

*Ah*___

p e legato

*8ve.*___

B

D Tempo I

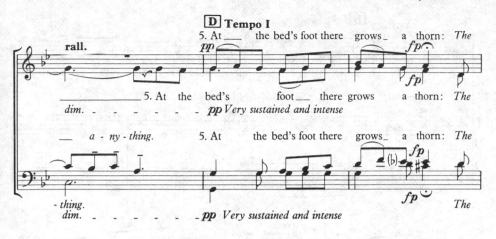

BARITONE
SOLO

6. Ov-er that bed_ the moon_ shines bright: *The bells_ of pa-ra-dise*

I heard them ring: De-no-ting our Sa-viour was born_ this night: *And I*

love____ my Lord Je-sus a - bove a-ny-thing.____

poco a poco rallentando

10. SHEPHERD'S PIPE CAROL

Words and music by
JOHN RUTTER

Available separately (X167)

Also available in the following arrangements:
1) S.S.A.A. voices (W76)
2) Unison voices with optional descant (U133)
3) Unison voices with easy accompaniment, shortened and simplified (U141)
4) Solo voice with slightly simplified accompaniment (Oxford Solo Songs)

© Oxford University Press 1967

C

mp dolce e legato

S. 3. 'None may hear my pipes on these hills so lone - ly

A. *p* Ah

T. *p* Ah

B. Piano *p* Ah

On the way to Beth - le - hem;— But a King will hear me—

Ah———— Ah————

Ah———— Ah————

Ah————————

play sweet lul - la - bies When I get to Beth - le - hem.'————

cresc. _ _ _

Ah———— *cresc. _ _ _*

Ah———— *cresc. _ _ _*

Ah———— *cresc. _ _ _*

5. 'May I come with you, shep-herd boy pi - ping mer - ri - ly,

Come with you to Beth - le - hem?___

Pay my hom- age too at the new King's cra - dle,

born this night in low - ly___ sta - ble yon - der,

Born for you at Beth - - - le - hem.'___

11. HAIL! BLESSED VIRGIN MARY

Words by
G. R. WOODWARD

Italian carol
arranged by CHARLES WOOD

1. Hail! Bless-ed Vir-gin Ma - ry! For so when
2. A - ve, a - ve Ma - ri - a! To glad-den
3. Arch - an-gels chant O - san - na, And Ho - ly,

he did meet thee, Spake migh-ty Ga - bri - el, And thus we greet
priest and peo - ple, The an-ge-lus shall ring from ev-'ry stee
Ho-ly, Ho - ly, Be-fore the In-fant born of thee, thou low -

thee. Come weal, come woe, Our hymn shall nev-er va - ry.
-ple. To sound his Vir-gin birth, Al-le-lu - i - a!
-ly, Aye-mai-den child of Jo-a-chim and An - na;

Hail! Bless-ed Vir-gin Ma - ry! Hail! Bless-ed Vir-gin Ma - ry!
A-ve, a-ve Ma-ri - a! A-ve, a-ve Ma-ri - a!
Arch-an-gels chant O-san - na. Arch-an-gels chant O-san - na.

Reprinted from *An Italian Carol Book* by permission of The Faith Press, Ltd.

© The Faith Press 1920

12. HERE WE COME A-WASSAILING

English traditional carol
arranged by JOHN RUTTER

From *Twelve Christmas Carols* (Set 1)

© Oxford University Press 1969

beg   from door   to   door,_____   But   we   are neigh - bours'

8ve -

child - ren Whom you have seen be - fore: *Love and   joy   come to*

you,   And to   you your   was - sail   too,   And God

8ve -

bless   you, and   send_ you a   hap - py New Year,   And God

ALL VOICES

send you a hap - py New Year._____ 4. Call

up the but - ler of this house, Put on his gold - en

ring;___ Let him bring us up a glass of beer, And

bet - ter we shall sing *Love and joy come to you,___ And to*

you your was-sail too,__ And God bless_ you, and send_ you a

hap - py New Year,_And God send_ you a hap - py New

Year.

mf espress.

5. We have got a lit-tle purse Of stretch-ing lea-ther skin; ____ We want a lit-tle of your mon-ey To line it well with- -in: *Love and joy come to you,___ And to you your was-sail*

too,__ And God bless you, and send__ you a hap - py New

Year, And God send you a hap - py New Year.

F

SOPRANOS *f*

ALTOS *Ah* _____ *Ah* _____

TENORS and BASSES *f*

6. Bring us out a ta - ble, And spread it with a cloth;

8ve - - - - - - - - -

f

8ve - - -   *8ve* - - -

Bring   us   out   a   moul - dy cheese,   And some of your Christ - mas

Love_ and   joy_____   come_ to

Love   and   joy_____   come   to

loaf: *Love and   joy   come   to   you,   And   to   you your was - sail*

you,____ And God send_____ you   a

you,   And God send_____ you   a

too,   And God bless____ you,   and   send__ you   a   hap - py New

8ve.- -

dim. - - - - - - mf

hap - py New Year,__And God send__ you   a   hap - py New   Year.__7. God

dim. - - - - mf

hap - py New Year,__And God send   you   a   hap - py New   Year. 7. God

dim. - - - - mf

Year,   And God send   you   a   hap - py New   Year._____ 7. God

p

(8ve) - - - - - - - - - - - - - - - - -

TENORS and BASSES

p

8. Good mas – ter and good mis – tress, While you're sit – ting by the fire, ___ Pray think of us poor child – ren Who are wand – 'ring in the

BASSES ONLY

mire: *Love and joy come to you, And to you your was – sail*

pp

too, And God bless you, and send_ you a hap - py New

Year, And God send you a hap - py New

Year.

13. A NEW YEAR CAROL

★Words anon.

BENJAMIN BRITTEN

1. Here we bring new wa-ter from the well___ so clear,
2. Sing__ reign of Fair__ Maid, with gold up-on her toe,
3. Sing__ reign of Fair__ Maid, with gold up-on her chin,

For to wor-ship God with, this hap-py New Year.
O-pen you the West Door, and turn the Old Year go.
O-pen you the East Door, and let the New Year in.

Sing

★From *Tom Tiddler's Ground* — Walter de la Mare

Reprinted by permission of Boosey and Hawkes Music Publishers Ltd., London

© Boosey & Co. Ltd. 1936

REFRAIN (for verses 1 & 2)

le-vy dew, sing le-vy dew, the wa-ter and the wine; The

se-ven bright gold wires and the bu-gles that do shine.

D.S. 𝄋

REFRAIN (for verse 3)

rall. molto

le-vy dew, sing le-vy dew, the wa-ter and the wine; The

una corda

se-ven bright gold wires and the bu-gles that do shine.

c

14. HOW FAR IS IT TO BETHLEHEM?

Words by
FRANCES CHESTERTON

English traditional melody
arranged by DAVID WILLCOCKS

Words reprinted by permission of A. P. Watt & Son
Also available separately (W92)

© Oxford University Press 1970

5. Great kings have pre - cious gifts, And we have naught, Lit - tle smiles and

5. Great kings have pre - cious gifts, And we have naught, Lit - tle smiles and

lit - tle tears Are all___ we brought. 6. For all wea - ry chil - dren

tears___ Are all___ we brought. 6. For all wea - ry chil - dren

(6.) Ma - ry must weep. Here, on his bed of straw
(7.) Babes in the byre, Sleep, as they sleep who find

(6.) Ma - ry must weep.___ Here, on___ his bed of straw___
(7.) Babes in the byre,___ Sleep, as___ they sleep who find___

Fine

Sleep, chil - dren, sleep. 7. God in his mo - ther's arms,
Their heart's de - sire.

Sleep,___ chil - dren, sleep. 7. God in his mo - ther's arms,
Their ___ heart's ___ de - sire.

15. MATIN RESPONSORY

Words translated from the
First Responsory of Advent Sunday
in the Office of Matins
(early medieval Roman rite)

Adapted from a Magnificat
by PALESTRINA
(as sung at the Advent Carol Services
in King's College Chapel, Cambridge)

© Oxford University Press 1970

SECOND BOY

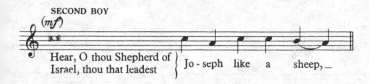

Hear, O thou Shepherd of Israel, thou that leadest } Jo-seph like a sheep,—

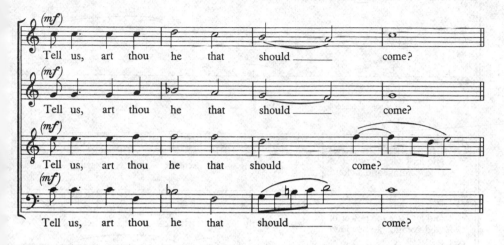

Tell us, art thou he that should _____ come?

Tell us, art thou he that should _____ come?

Tell us, art thou he that should come? _____

Tell us, art thou he that should _____ come?

FULL BOYS

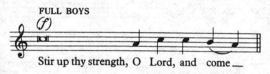

Stir up thy strength, O Lord, and come—

to reign over thy peo - ple Is - ra - - el.

to reign over thy peo - ple—— Is - - - ra - el. _____

to reign over thy peo - ple Is - ra - - - - - el.

to reign over thy peo - ple Is - ra - - el. _____

CANTOR

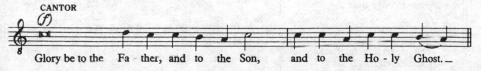

Glory be to the Fa - ther, and to the Son, and to the Ho - ly Ghost. —

16. COME, THOU REDEEMER OF THE EARTH

(Veni, Redemptor gentium)

ST AMBROSE (340–397)
tr. J. M. NEALE and others

Traditional melody
adapted by M. PRAETORIUS (1571–1621)
arranged by DAVID WILLCOCKS

Also available separately (*Six Christmas Hymns* arr. David Willcocks)

★ Verse 1 may be sung unaccompanied.

Ⓒ Oxford University Press 1970

VERSES 2–7★

CHOIR
and
ORGAN

2. Be - got - ten of __ no hu - man __ will, But of __ the
3. The vir - gin womb that bur - den __ gained With vir - gin

Spi - rit, thou __ art __ still The __ Word __ of God ___ in __
ho - nour all __ un - stained; The __ ban - ners there __ of __

flesh __ ar - rayed, ___ The pro - mised fruit __ to man __ dis - played.
vir - tue __ glow; God in __ his tem - ple dwells __ be - low.

4. Forth from his chamber goeth he,
That royal home of purity,
A giant in twofold substance one,
Rejoicing now his course to run.

6. O equal to thy Father, thou!
Gird on thy fleshly mantle now;
The weakness of our mortal state
With deathless might invigorate.

5. From God the Father he proceeds,
To God the Father back he speeds;
His course he runs to death and hell,
Returning on God's throne to dwell.

7. Thy cradle here shall glitter bright,
And darkness breathe a newer light,
Where endless faith shall shine serene,
And twilight never intervene.

★ Verses 2 and 3 may be omitted.

★ Alternative version of v. 8 (as given in *The English Hymnal*)

17. IL EST NÉ LE DIVIN ENFANT

(Born on earth the divine Christ Child)

English words by
JACQUELINE FROOM

French traditional carol
arranged by **JOHN RUTTER**

From *Eight Christmas Carols* (Set 1)

© Oxford University Press 1967

TENORS *mp*

-vè - ne - ment. / 1. De - puis plus de qua - tre mille ans
Sa - viour mild. / *1.'Tis four thou - sand_ years and more*

Nous le pro - met -taient les pro - phè - tes, De - puis plus de qua-
*Men his birth have been pro - phe - sy - ing; 'Tis four thou - sand_*

poco rit.

-tre mille ans _ Nous at - ten - dions cet heur - eux temps.
years and more_ While we longed for the joys in store.

B **a tempo**
p
S.
A.

Il est né le di - vin en - fant, Jou - ez haut-bois, ré - son -
*Born on earth the di - vine Christ Child, O - boes, re - joice, with_*

fp   *p*

T.
B.
fp   *fp*

fp (T.B. hum)

B **a tempo**

p

Jou - ez haut-bois,   ré - son - nez mu - set — tes;   Il est né   le di -
O - boes, re - joice,   with_ bag - pipes   vy — ing;   Born on earth   the di -

- ez   haut - bois,   ré - son - nez   mu - set — tes;
o - boes, re - joice,   with   bag - - - pipes   vy — ing;

- vin en - fant,   Chan - tons tous son a - vè - ne - ment.
- vine Christ Child,   Sing   to_ wel - come the   Sa - viour mild.

Chan - tons   son a - vè - ne - ment.
Come   wel - - - come the   Sa - viour mild.

TENORS and BASSES   *mp legato*

3. Une é - ta - ble est son loge - ment,
3. In   a   sta - ble ___ here   on   earth,

Un   peu de paille est ___ sa cou - chet - te;   Une é - ta - ble est
Je - sus, ___ in   the ___ man - ger   ly - ing,   In   a   sta - ble ___

son loge - ment,   Pour   un   Dieu   quel ___   a - baisse - ment!
here   on   earth,   O   how   low - ly   our   Sa - viour's birth!

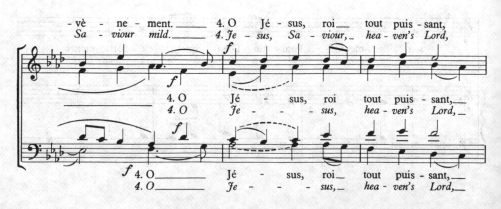

18. I SAW A MAIDEN

Words 15th century (adapted)

Old Basque Noël
with refrain added by
EDGAR PETTMAN

1. I   saw a mai - den sit - ten and sing: She lull - ed a child, a swee - te Lord - ing.
2. This ve - ry Lord he made al - le thing: Of lord - es the Lord, of king - es the King.
3. There was mick-le me - lo - dy at that child-es birth: And all in hea-ven's bliss, they ma - de mick-le mirth.
4. An - gels sang that night and said - en to that child: Now blest be thou and she, both meek and mild.
5. Pray we to that child and to his mo - ther dear, His bless - ing to them that mak - en now cheer.

Lul - lay, lul - lay, my dear son, my sweet - ing. Lul - lay, lul - lay, my dear heart, my own dear dar - ling.

Alternative version of text (as given in *The University Carol Book*)

1. I saw a maiden sitting and sing,
   She lull'd her child a little Lording.

   Lullay, lullay, my dear son, my sweeting.
   Lullay, lullay, my dear son, my own dear dearing.

2. This very Lord, He made all things,
   And this very God, the King of all Kings.

3. There was sweet music at this child's birth,
   And heaven filled with angels, making much mirth.

4. Heaven's angels sang to welcome the child
   Now born of a maid, all undefiled.

5. Pray we and sing on this festal day,
   That peace may dwell with us alway.

Reprinted from *The University Carol Book* by permission of H. Freeman & Co.

19. MYN LYKING

Words 15th century

R. R. TERRY

The words of this carol are taken from the Sloane MS. : spellings are unaltered.
Reprinted by permission of J. Curwen & Sons Ltd.

To my mother

20. I SING OF A MAIDEN

Words traditional

PATRICK HADLEY

SOPRANO I · SOPRANO II · PIANO

I sing of a mai-den That is make-less; King of all kings

To her son she ches. He came all so still Where his mo-ther was, As dew in A-pril That fall-eth on the

© The Year Book Press, Ltd. 1936. Reprinted by permission of Ascherberg, Hopwood & Crew, Ltd.

21. IT CAME UPON THE MIDNIGHT CLEAR

Words by
E. H. SEARS

Traditional English tune
adapted by ARTHUR SULLIVAN
Descant and organ part by
DAVID WILLCOCKS

In moderate time (♩ = 92)

SOPRANO
ALTO

1. It __ came up-on the __ mid-night clear, That glo-rious song of old,
2. Still through the clo-ven __ skies they come, With peace-ful wings un-furled;
3. Yet __ with the woes of __ sin and strife The world has suf-fered long;

TENOR
BASS

From an-gels bend-ing near the earth To __ touch their harps of gold:
And still their heav'n-ly mu-sic floats O'er __ all __ the wea-ry world;
Be-neath the an-gel-strain have rolled Two __ thou-sand years of wrong;

'Peace on the earth, good-will to men, From heav'n's all-gra-cious King!'
A-bove its sad and low-ly plains They bend on ho-v'ring wing;
And man, at war with man, hears not The love-song which they bring:

The world in so-lemn still-ness __ lay To __ hear __ the an-gels sing.
And ev-er o'er its __ Ba-bel __ sounds The __ bless-ed an-gels sing.
O hush the noise, ye __ men of __ strife, And __ hear __ the an-gels sing!

Also available separately (*Six Christmas Hymns* arr. David Willcocks)

© Oxford University Press 1970

(to next page for v. 4)

22. THE CHERRY TREE CAROL

English traditional carol
arranged by DAVID WILLCOCKS

Also available separately (X197)

© Oxford University Press 1970

1st SOPRANOS

p 3. O then be-spoke Ma - ry, With words both meek and mild,
mf 5. Then bowed down the high-est tree Un - to__ our La - dy's hand;

2nd SOPRANOS

V. 3: *pp* Ah_____   Ah
V. 5: *mp*

ALTOS

V. 3: *pp* Ah   Ah____
V. 5: *mp*

'Pluck me__ one cher-ry, Jo - seph; For__ that I am with child.'____
'See,' Ma-ry cried, 'see,__ Jo - seph, I have cher-ries at com - mand.'____

TENORS *mp*

Ah

BARITONES *mf*

4.   'Go to the tree then, Ma - ry, And it__ shall bow to thee;   And
6. 'O eat your cher-ries, Ma - ry, O__ eat__ your cher-ries now;   O

BASSES *mp*

Ah

after v. 6: D.C. for v. 7

Ah

you shall ga - ther cher - ries By__ one, by two, by three.'____
eat your cher-ries, Ma - ry, That grow up-on the bough.' ____

23. MASTERS IN THIS HALL

Words by
WILLIAM MORRIS

French traditional carol
arranged by DAVID WILLCOCKS

1. Mas-ters in this hall, Hear ye news to-day Brought from ov-er sea, And ev-er I you pray:

REFRAIN for vv. 1—7★
v. 1: ALL VOICES
vv. 2, 4, 5: S. and A.
vv. 3, 6, 7: T. and B.

Now-ell! Now-ell! Now - ell! Now-ell sing we clear! Holp-en are all folk on earth, Born is God's Son so dear:

★The dynamic level of the refrain is in each case the same as that of the verse preceding it.
Also available separately (X208)

© Oxford University Press 1970

SOPRANOS and ALTOS

mp 2. Go - ing o'er the hills,_____ Through the milk - white snow,_____
mf 4. Quoth I, 'Fel - lows mine,_____ Why this guise sit ye?
mf 5. 'Shep- herds should of right_____ Leap and dance and sing,_____

mp

D.S. for REFRAIN

Heard I ew - es bleat_____ While the wind did blow:
Mak - ing but dull cheer,_____ Shep - herds though ye be?'
Thus to see ye sit,_____ Is a right strange thing':

TENORS and BASSES

pp 3. Shep- herds ma - ny an one_____ Sat a - mong the sheep,_____
mf 6. Quoth these fel - lows then,_____ 'To Beth - lem town we go,_____ To

v. 3: *pp*
v. 6: *mp*

D.S. for REFRAIN

No man spake more word_____ Than they had been a - sleep:
see a might - y lord_____ Lie in man - ger low':

(ALL VOICES)

Now-ell! Now-ell! Now - ell! Now-ell sing we clear! Holp - en

S. are all folk on earth, __ Born __ is God's Son so dear: _____ Now-

A. are all folk on earth, __ Born __ is God's Son so dear: _____

T. are all folk on earth, __ Born __ is God's Son so dear: _____ Now-

B. are all folk on earth, __ Born __ is God's Son so dear: _____

24. NOËL NOUVELET

(Nowell, sing nowell)

English words by JOHN RUTTER

French traditional carol
arranged by JOHN RUTTER

From *Twelve Christmas Carols* (Set 2)

© Oxford University Press 1969

- em trou - ve - rez l'ag - ne - let.' No - ël nou - ve -
Lamb   of   God, love's own pure ray.'   No - well, sing no -

poco rall.   **a tempo**

- let,   No - ël chan - tons i - ci.
- well   good   peo - ple   ga - thered   here.

p

C *mp dolce*

S.
A.

S.A. { 3. En___ Beth - lé - em,   é - tant tous___ ré - u - nis,___
only { *3. When to Beth - le - hem   they   came in___ low - ly   fear,*

T.
B.

p (T.B. sing "Aw")
(Piano tacet)

Trou - vent l'en - fant,___   Jo - seph, Ma - rie aus - si.
Found they gen - tle   Ma - ry___   with her___ son so   dear.

S. La crèche é - tait   au   lieu d'un ber - ce - let,
Heav'n's might-y   Lord   all   cra - dled   in   the   hay,

A. La crèche é - tait   au   lieu   d'un   ber - ce - let,
Heav'n's might-y   Lord   all   cra - dled   in   the   hay,

D

S.A. No - ël nou - ve - let,   No - ël chan-tons i - ci.
No-well, sing no - well,   good   peo - ple— ga-thered here.

mp   *p*

TENORS and BASSES *mf*

4. Bien - tôt les   rois,   par   l'é-toile é - clair - cis
4. *East-ern sa - ges   seek him,   in   the dark-ness drear*

mp

dim.   *p*

De— l'o - rient dont   ils é - taient sor - tis   A Beth-lé-
By a star il - lu - mined   shin-ing forth so   clear,   Guid - ing—

p

25. SANS DAY CAROL

Cornish traditional carol
arranged by JOHN RUTTER

Words collated by Percy Dearmer and used by permission of Oxford University Press
Arrangement from *Twelve Christmas Carols* (Set 2)

© Oxford University Press 1969

first tree in the green- wood, it was the hol - ly, hol - ly, hol -

- ly! And the first tree in the green - wood, it was the hol -

- ly!

TENORS and
BASSES   *mp*   **B**

2. Now the hol - ly bears a ber - ry as green as the grass, And

ALL VOICES

Ma - ry bore_ Je - sus, who died on the cross: And_

Je-sus Christ
Ma - ry bore_ Je - sus our Sa - viour for to be,_____ And the

first_ tree in the green-wood, it was the hol - ly,_____ hol - ly,_____ hol -

- ly! And the first tree in the green - wood, it_ was_ the_ hol - ly!

(Piano tacet)

C

E

cresc.   *f*

trust we our Sa - viour, who rose from the dead: And

mf

Je - sus Christ

dim.   *mf*

S. *And the*

Ma - ry bore Je - sus our Sa - viour for to be,

A. *Ah*
T. *Ah*
B.

dim.   *mf*

first tree in the green - wood, it was the hol - ly,

mp *Ah*

T. *hol -*
mf
mp

B. *Ah*

mp

p

26. SIR CHRISTÈMAS

Words anon. (*c.* 1500)

WILLIAM MATHIAS

Also available separately (X207)

This carol is from *Ave Rex*, a carol sequence by William Mathias (O.U.P.) commissioned by the Cardiff Polyphonic Choir.

© Oxford University Press 1970

No-well, no-well,   no-well, no-well?

ƒ I   am here, Sir Chris - tè - mas, Sir

Chris - tè - mas, Sir Chris - tè - mas.

Wel-come, my lord— Sir Chris - tè - mas!

Sw. ƒ

Man.

Wel-come to   all,— both more and less, Come near,   come near,   come

Where-fore sing we at a__ brayde:

No-well, no-well, no-well, no-well,

Gt.

Ped.

no-well, no-well, no-well, no-well.

B

Bu - vez bien, bu - vez bien par

B

tou - te la com - pag - nie.__ (e)

Make good cheer and be right mer-ry, And

sing with us now joy-ful-ly,_____ joy-ful-ly,_____ joy-ful-ly:

No-well, no-well,   no-well, no-well,   no-well, no-well, no-well, no-well,   no-

-well! _____

(shout)

No - well!

Man.   **Ped.**

27. O COME, O COME, EMMANUEL

(Veni, veni, Emmanuel)

Words 18th century
tr. T. A. LACEY

Melody from 15th century
French Franciscan Processional★
adapted and arranged by
DAVID WILLCOCKS

Also available separately (*Six Christmas Hymns* arr. David Willcocks)

★Paris, Bib. Nat. Fonds Latin MS. 10581
Congregation should sing sections marked ⌐ ⌐ of verses 1, 2, 4 and 5.
© Oxford University Press 1970   Words from *The English Hymnal* by permission of Oxford University Press

VERSES 2 and 4
TENORS and BASSES

f 2. O come, thou Branch of Jes - se! draw The quar - ry from the li - on's claw; From

f 4. O come, thou Lord of Da - vid's Key! The roy - al door fling wide and free; Safe-

Full Sw. *p*

Ped.

T.

the dread ca - verns of the grave, From ne - ther hell, thy peo - ple save. Re-

B.

the dread ca - verns of the grave, From ne - ther hell, thy peo - ple save. Re-

- guard for us the heav'n - ward road, And bar the way to death's a - bode. Re-

- guard for us the heav'n - ward road, And bar the way to death's a - bode. Re-

cresc.

REFRAIN

f

after v. 2: straight on for v. 3
after v. 4: D.C. for v. 5

- joice! Re - joice! Em - ma - nu - el Shall come to thee, O Is - ra - el.

- joice! Re - joice! Em - ma - nu - el Shall come to thee, O Is - ra - el.

after v. 2: straight on for v. 3
after v. 4: D.C. for v. 5

VERSE 3

mf SOPRANOS and ALTOS

3. O come, O come, thou Day - spring bright! Pour on our souls thy heal - ing light; Dis -

Ch. flutes *p*

(Man.)

S.

cresc.

REFRAIN *f*

- pel the long night's lin - g'ring gloom, And pierce the sha-dows of ___ the tomb. Re -

A.

cresc.

f

- pel the long night's lin - g'ring gloom, And pierce the sha-dows of ___ the tomb. Re -

cresc.

f

Back to p. 121 for v. 4

Em - ma - nu - el Shall come to thee, O Is - ra - el.

- joice! Re - joice! Em - ma - nu - el Shall come to thee, O Is - ra - el.

- joice! Re - joice! Em - ma - nu - el Shall come to thee, O Is - ra - el.

Back to p. 121 for v. 4

28. THE SHEPHERDS' CRADLE SONG
(*Wiegenlied*)

Tr. A. FOXTON FERGUSON

KARL LEUNER
arranged by
CHARLES MACPHERSON

Andante moderato e teneramente

SOPRANO: O sleep thou heav'n-born trea - sure, thou, Sleep sound, thou dear - est child; _____ White an - gel wings _ shall fan thy brow With breez - es soft _ and mild. _____ We shepherds poor are here to sing A

ALTO: O sleep thou heav'n-born trea - sure, thou, Sleep sound, thou dear - est child; White an - - - - gel wings shall fan _ thy brow _ With breez - es soft and mild. _____ We shepherds poor are here to sing A

TENOR: O sleep _ thou heav'n-born trea - sure, thou, Sleep sound, thou dear - est, dear - est child; White an - gel wings _ shall fan _ thy brow _ With breez - es soft and mild. _____ We shepherds poor are here _ to sing _ A

BASS: O sleep thou heav'n-born trea - sure, thou, Sleep sound, thou dear - est, dear - est child; White an - gel wings shall fan thy brow _ With breez - es soft and mild. We shep - herds poor _ are _ here to sing _ A

© J. Curwen & Sons, Ltd., 1912. Reprinted by permission

29. OF THE FATHER'S HEART BEGOTTEN
(Corde natus ex parentis)

Melody from 'Piae Cantiones,
Theoderici Petri Nylandensis', 1582
arranged by
DAVID WILLCOCKS

PRUDENTIUS (*b.* 348)
tr. R. F. DAVIS

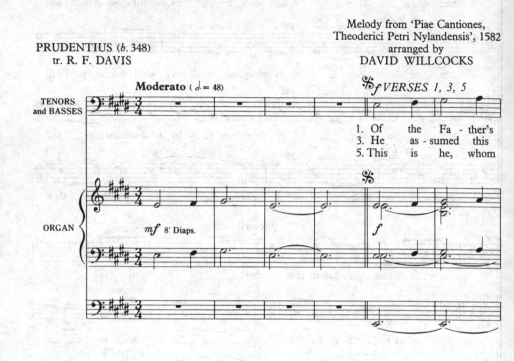

TENORS
and BASSES

VERSES 1, 3, 5

1. Of the Fa - ther's
3. He as - sumed this
5. This is he, whom

ORGAN

mf 8' Diaps.

heart be - got - ten, Ere the world from cha - os rose,
mor - tal bo - dy, Frail and fee - ble, doomed to die,
seer and sy - bil Sang in a - ges long gone by;

Words reprinted by permission of J. M. Dent & Sons, Ltd.
Also available separately (E100)

© Oxford University Press 1963

He is Al - pha: from that Foun - tain   All that is and hath been
That the race from dust cre - a - ted   Might not per - ish ut - ter -
This is he of old re - veal - ed   In the page of pro - phe -

flows;   He is O - me - ga, of all   things   Yet to
- ly,   Which the dread - ful Law had sen - tenced   In the
- cy;   Lo! he comes, the pro - mised Sa - viour;   Let the

after vv. 1 and 3: straight on for vv. 2 and 4
after v. 5: to p. 131 for v. 6

come the mys - tic Close,
depths of hell to lie,   *Ev - er - more and ev - er - more.*
world his prais - es cry!

E

VERSES 2, 4

SOPRANOS (and ALTOS)

2. By his word was all cre - a - ted; He com - mand - ed and _ 'twas
4. O how blest that won - drous birth - day, When the Maid the curse _ re-

Man.   *mf* 8', 4' flutes

done;   Earth and sky and bound - less o - cean,   U - ni - verse of
-trieved,   Brought to birth man - kind's sal - va - tion,   By the Ho - ly

three _ in one,   All that sees the moon's soft ra - - - - - diance,
Ghost _ con - ceived;   And the Babe, the world's Re - deem - - - - er,

D.S. for vv. 3 and 5

All that breathes be - neath the sun,   *Ev - er - more and ev - er - more.*
In her lov - ing arms re - ceived,

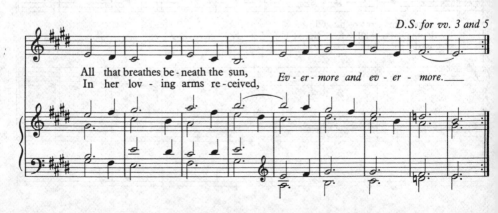

VERSE 6

CHOIR I and CONGREGATION

6. Sing, ye heights of heav'n, his prais - es;

CHOIR II

S.A.

6. Sing, sing his prais - es;

T.B.

ORGAN

An - gels and Arch - an - gels, sing! Where - so -

An - gels and Arch - an - gels, sing! Where - so -

sonore

30. THE TWELVE DAYS OF CHRISTMAS

English traditional carol★
arranged by JOHN RUTTER

Adapted from the arrangement in *Eight Christmas Carols* (Set 2).
Audience may sing melody line during sections marked ⌐ ⌐.

★ Melody for "Five gold rings" added by Frederic Austin, and reproduced by
permission of Novello & Co. Ltd.

© Oxford University Press 1970

fourth day of Christ-mas my true love sent to me Four call-ing birds,

three French hens, two tur-tle doves and a par-tridge in a pear

tree. On the fifth day of Christ-mas my true love sent to me

five   gold___   rings,_____   four __ call - ing birds, three French hens,

two__ tur - tle doves and a   par - tridge in a pear   tree.   On the

7

sev'nth   day   of Christ - mas   my   true love sent   to   me

Sev'n swans a-swim-ming, six geese a-lay-ing, five gold____ rings,_____ four____ call-ing birds, three French hens, two____ tur-tle doves and a par-tridge in a pear tree. On the

par - tridge in a pear tree.   On the ninth day of Christ-mas my

mf   **9**

mf

mf

true·love sent to me   Nine la - dies danc-ing, eight maids a-milk-ing,

ritmico

sev'n swans a-swim-ming, six geese a - lay -ing,   five   gold__

five gold _ rings, _____ four _ call-ing birds, three French hens,

molto allargando

two tur - tle doves and a par - tridge in a pear tree.   On the

12 **Maestoso**

twelfth day of Christ - mas my true love sent to me

Maestoso

Tempo I (fast)

six geese a - lay - ing, five gold rings,

four call - ing birds, three French hens,

two turtle doves and a par - tridge in a pear tree.

31. ONCE IN ROYAL DAVID'S CITY

Words by
C. F. ALEXANDER

H. J. GAUNTLETT
Vv. 1—5 harmonised by A. H. MANN
Descant and organ part by DAVID WILLCOCKS

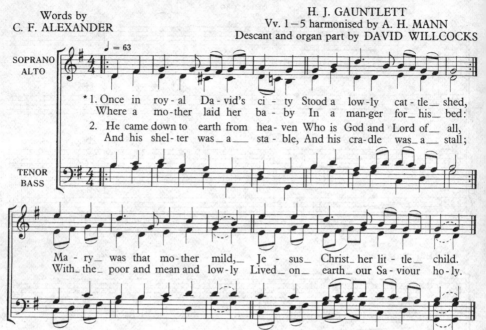

*1. Once in roy-al Da-vid's ci-ty Stood a low-ly cat-tle shed,
Where a mo-ther laid her ba-by In a man-ger for his bed:
2. He came down to earth from hea-ven Who is God and Lord of all,
And his shel-ter was a sta-ble, And his cra-dle was a stall;

Ma-ry was that mo-ther mild, Je-sus Christ her lit-tle child.
With the poor and mean and low-ly Lived on earth our Sa-viour ho-ly.

3. And through all his wondrous childhood
   He would honour and obey,
Love and watch the lowly maiden,
   In whose gentle arms he lay:
Christian children all must be
Mild, obedient, good as he.

4. For he is our childhood's pattern,
   Day by day like us he grew,
He was little, weak, and helpless,
   Tears and smiles like us he knew:
And he feeleth for our sadness,
And he shareth in our gladness.

5. And our eyes at last shall see him,
   Through his own redeeming love,
For that child so dear and gentle
   Is our Lord in heaven above;
And he leads his children on
To the place where he is gone.

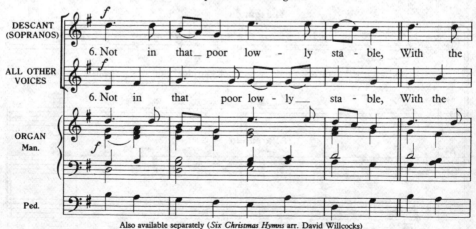

DESCANT (SOPRANOS)

6. Not in that poor low-ly sta-ble, With the

ALL OTHER VOICES

6. Not in that poor low-ly sta-ble, With the

ORGAN Man.

Ped.

Also available separately (*Six Christmas Hymns* arr. David Willcocks)
* The first verse may be sung by a solo treble.
Harmonisation for vv. 1—5 reprinted by permission of Novello & Co. Ltd.
© Oxford University Press 1970 (descant and organ part)

for Michael Nicholas and the Choir of St. Matthew's Church, Northampton

32. OUT OF YOUR SLEEP

Words: 15th century, anon.

RICHARD RODNEY BENNETT

1. Out of your sleep a - rise and wake, For

God man - kind now hath y - take. All of a maid with -

- out a - ny make; Of all wo - men she bear - eth the bell.

2. And through a mai - dè fair and wise, Now man is made of

full great price; Now an - gels kne - len to man's

No. 2 of *Five Carols*, reprinted by permission of Universal Edition

© Universal Edition (London) Ltd., London 1967

ser - vice, And at this time all this be - fell. 3. Now

man is bright - er than the sun; Now

man in heav'n on high shall won; Bless - èd be God this

game is be - gun And his mo - ther the Em - press of hell.

4. That ev - er was thrall now is he free; That ev - er was small now

great is she; Now shall God deem both thee and me Un - to his

bliss_ if we do_ well._ 5. Now man he may to hea-ven wend; Now

heav'n and earth to him they bend. He that was foe_ now is our_ friend. This

is no nay_ that I you_ tell._ 6. Now bless-èd Bro-ther

grant_ us grace, At doom-ès day to see_ thy face, And in thy

court_ to have a place, That we may there_ sing thee no-well.

33. PAST THREE A CLOCK

Words by G. R. WOODWARD
(refrain traditional)

English traditional carol
arranged by JOHN RUTTER

Arrangement from *Twelve Christmas Carols* (Set 2)

Words, from *The Cambridge Carol Book*, are reprinted by permission of the S.P.C.K.

© Oxford University Press 1969

morn - ing: Past three a clock; Good mor-row, mas-ters all!

mp SEMI-CHORUS   *cresc.* _ _ _

2. Se-raph quire sing - eth, An-gel-bell ring-eth: Hark_ how_ they_

CHOIR
p

S.
A.   Sing "Ah"   *cresc.*

T.
B.

p (Piano *ad lib.*)   *cresc.*

_ _ _ _ _ _ _ _ *f*   **B**
                                       mp

rime   it, Time it, and chime it. Past three a clock, And a

mf   dim.   *p*

mf   dim.   *p*

(SEMI-CHORUS
rejoin others)

cold fros-ty morn - ing: Past three a clock; Good mor-row, mas-ters all!

3. Mid earth re - joi - ces Hear-ing such voi-ces Ne'er-to-fore_ so_ well

voi - ces

Ca - rol - ling Now-ell. Past three a clock, And a cold_ fros - ty_

morn - ing: Past three a clock; Good mor-row, mas - ters all.

p well sustained

6. Myrrh from full — cof - fer   In - cense they of - fer:

p well sustained
(Piano tacet)   of - fer:

Nor — is — the — gold - en   nug - get with - hold - en.

F *pp*   *legato*

Past three a   clock,   And a   cold — fros - ty — morn - ing: Past three a

pp   *legato*

pp

legato   *mf*

clock;   Good mor-row, mas - ters   all!   7. Thus they: I

f

legato   7. Thus they: I   pray   you,

mf

34. PERSONENT HODIE

Words from *Piae Cantiones*, 1582

German, 1360
arranged by GUSTAV HOLST

Reprinted by permission of J. Curwen & Sons, Ltd.
For English words, see *The Oxford Book of Carols*
'Bethlehem adeunt' has been substituted for 'Parvulum inquirunt' (which may well be
a clerical error since no similar repetition of words is to be found in the other verses.)

© Gustav Holst 1924

35. QUELLE EST CETTE ODEUR AGRÉABLE?

(Whence is that goodly fragrance flowing?)

Tr. A. B. RAMSAY
(v. 4 tr. DAVID WILLCOCKS)

French traditional carol
arranged by DAVID WILLCOCKS

v. 1: SOPRANOS (and ALTOS)
v. 2: TENORS (and BASSES)

English words of vv. 1–3 reprinted by permission of the Master and Fellows of Magdalene College, Cambridge

Also available separately (X209)

© Oxford University Press 1970

des fleurs du prin-temps? Quelle est cette o - deur a - gré -
flow - 'ry fields in May, Whence is that good - ly fra - grance
- mais si ra - dieux? Mais quelle é - cla-tan - te lu -
climb the morn - ing skies! What is that light so bril - liant,

- a - ble, Ber-gers, qui ra - vit tous nos sens?
flow - ing, Steal-ing our sen - ses all a - - way?
- miè - re Dans la nuit vient frap - per nos yeux!
break - ing Here in the night a - cross our eyes?

3. A Beth-lé - em, __ dans __ u - ne __ crè - che, Il vient de vous __ naî -
3. Beth-le - hem! there __ in __ man - ger __ ly - ing, Find your Re - deem - er, __

- tre un Sau - veur; Al - lons, que rien __ ne __ vous em - pê - che;
haste a - way, Run ye __ with ea - ger __ foot-steps __ hie - ing!

D'a - do - rer vo - tre___ Ré - demp - teur. A Beth - lé - em,___ dan
Wor - ship the Sa - viour born___ to - day. Beth - le - hem! there___ in

u - ne crè - che, Il vient de vous___ naî - tre un Sau - veur.
man - ger ly - ing, Find your Re - deem - er,___ haste a - way.

BARITONE SOLO
f ma dolce

4. Dieu tout-puis-sant, gloire é - ter - nel - le Vous soit ren - du - e
4. Praise to the Lord of all cre - a - tion, Glo - ry to God the

Ah___   Ah___

Ah___   Ah___

jus - qu'aux cieux; Que la paix soit u - ni - ver - sel - le,
fount of grace; May peace a - bide in ev - 'ry na - tion,

Ah___

Que la grâce a - bonde en tous lieux. Dieu tout - puis -
Good - will in men of ev - 'ry race. Praise to the

dim.

Ah

- sant, gloire é - ter - nel - le Vous soit ren - du - e
Lord of all cre - a - tion, Glo - ry to God the

Ah   Ah

Ah   Ah

Ah   Ah

jus - qu'aux cieux.
fount of grace.

Solo stop

rit.

36. QUEM PASTORES LAUDAVERE

(Shepherds left their flocks a-straying)

German, 14th century
arranged by JOHN RUTTER

Tr. IMOGEN HOLST

English words reprinted by permission of G. & I. Holst Ltd.

Also available separately (X211)

© Oxford University Press 1970

Na - - tus est____ rex glo - - ri - ae.
'Christ____ is born____ in Beth - le - hem.'

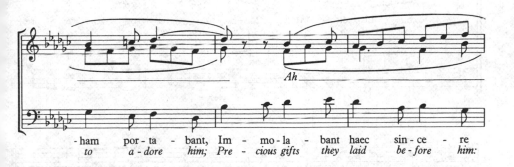

S. A.

Ah ____ Ah

T. and B.

2. Ad quem ma - gi am - bu - la - bant, Au - rum, thus, _ myrr -
2. Wise men came from far, _ and saw him: Knelt_ in 'hom - age

Ah ____

- ham por - ta - bant, Im - mo - la - bant haec sin - ce - re
to a - dore him; Pre - cious gifts they laid be - fore him:

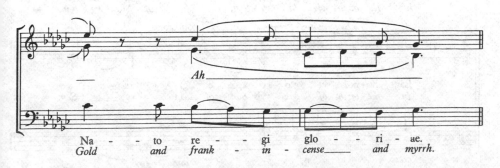

Ah ____

Na - - to re - gi glo - - ri - ae.
Gold and frank - in - cense____ and myrrh.

Note: v. 2 may be sung by three solo voices.

Note: Choir I part in v. 3 may be sung by a solo voice, in which case Choir II should sing "*Ah*"

37. QUITTEZ, PASTEURS
(Come leave your sheep)

English words by JOHN RUTTER

French traditional carol
arranged by JOHN RUTTER

From *Twelve Christmas Carols* (Set 1)

© Oxford University Press 1969

*A few sopranos and tenors, or solo voice

legato

le ver - rez ___ Cou - ché dans une é - ta - ble Comme un en -
li - eth there ___ with - in a low - ly man - ger; An in - fant

S.
A.
pp sempre

Sing "Ah"

T.
B.
pp sempre
(Piano tacet)

- fant Nu, pau - vre, lan - guis - sant; Re - con - nais - sez Son
poor He lan - guish - eth full sore. God's lov - ing care Hath

poco cresc. - - - - - - - - - **mp**

a - mour in - ef - fa - ble Pour nous ve - nir cher - cher Il
saved us all from dan - ger And brought us to his fold; Now

poco cresc. - - - - **p**

mf

est, il est, Il est ___ le fi - dèle ber - ger! Il
own, now own His faith - ful love re - vealed of old. Now

mp

est, il est, Il est___ le fi-dèle ber-ger!___
own, now own His faith-ful love re-vealed of old.___

TENORS and BASSES

3. Rois
3. Ye

legato

d'O- -rient L'é-toi-le vous é-clair -e; A
sa- -ges three Ar-rayed in roy-al splen-dour, Your

ce grand roi Ren-dez hom-mage et foi. L'as-tre bril-
ho- -mage pay; a king is born this day. The star ye

-frez l'or, la myrrhe et l'en - cens._____
*gifts are pre - cious in his sight.*_____

-frez l'or, la myrrhe et l'en - cens._____
*gifts are pre - cious in his sight.*_____

SOPRANOS *mp*

ALTOS

4. Es - prit___ di - vin   A
4. Come Ho - ly Ghost,   Of

TENORS

BASSES *mp*

A
Of

qui tout est pos - si - ble Per - cez nos coeurs___ De
bles - sings source e - ter - nal, Our souls in - spire___ With

(Piano tacet)

De
With

38. RESONEMUS LAUDIBUS

14th century carol★
arranged by DAVID WILLCOCKS

★ transcribed and edited by Frank Ll. Harrison (from *Now make we Merthe*, Bk. 1—O.U.P.)
Also available separately (X210)

© Oxford University Press 1970

39. THE ANGELS AND THE SHEPHERDS

Words adapted from
HELEN A. DICKINSON

Bohemian traditional carol
arranged by C. H. TREVOR

The angels

Moderato e leggiero (♩ = c. 80)

SOPRANOS

1. Shep - herds, O__ hark ye,__ glad_ ti - dings_ we__ bring,

poco rit.

Peace and__ good - will to__ the__ world now_ we__ sing;

Meno mosso

See in a man - ger Christ the An - oint - ed, Whom for your Sa - viour

Slow

God hath ap - point - ed. Al - le - lu - ia.

The shepherds

Poco meno mosso, leggiero

TENORS and
BASSES

2. In yon - der__ man - ger__ be - hold now_ he__ lies,

poco rit.

Whom an - gel - voi - ces__ fore - told from__ the__ skies.

Meno mosso

Seek - ing thy mer - cy, we kneel be - fore thee, Sing - ing thy prais - es,

Words used by permission of H. W. Gray Inc.

Also available separately (X 78)

© Oxford University Press 1961

Lento

hum - bly a - dore thee. *Al - le - lu - ia.*

The angels and the shepherds

Tempo primo

S.
A.
3. Still through the__ a - ges__ the__ song doth__ re - sound,

T.
B.
3. Still through__ a - ges doth re - sound,

Peace and__ good - will on __ the__ earth shall__ a - bound;

Peace,__ good - will on__ earth a - bound;

Meno mosso   *sempre mf*

Bear we the ti - dings to ev - 'ry na - tion, Born is the Christ Child

Al - le - lu - ia. Al - le -

Lento

for man's sal - va - tion. *Al - le - lu - ia.*

- lu - ia. Al - le - lu - ia.

40. SILENT NIGHT

Words by JOSEF MOHR,
tr. DAVID WILLCOCKS

FRANZ GRUBER
arranged by DAVID WILLCOCKS

© Oxford University Press 1970

This setting may more effectively be sung a semitone lower.

v. 1: straight on
v. 3: on to p. 187

SOPRANO

1. Sleep in hea - ven-ly peace.____
3. Christ th'in - car - nate God.____

A.

*Ah*____ *Ah*____

T.

ho - ly child.
- demp - tion and grace,

*Ah*____

B.

*Ah*____ *Ah* *Ah*

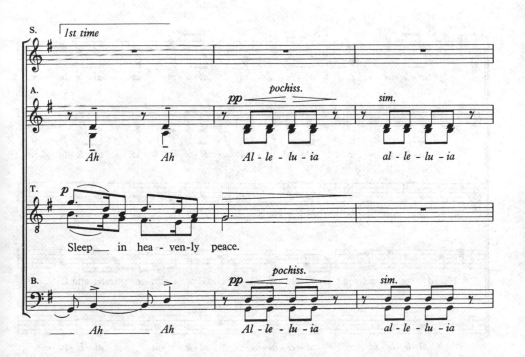

S.

1st time

A.

Ah *Ah* *Al - le - lu - ia* *al - le - lu - ia*

T.

Sleep__ in hea - ven-ly peace.

B.

__ *Ah*__ *Ah* *Al - le - lu - ia* *al - le - lu - ia*

dal ℅ for v. 3

Christ our Sa-viour is here,___ Christ our Sa-viour is here.___
Christ our Sa-viour is here,___ Christ our Sa-viour is here.___
Christ our Sa-viour is here,___ Christ our Sa-viour is here.___
Christ our Sa-viour is here,___ Christ our Sa-viour is here.___
Christ our Sa-viour is here, Christ our Sa-viour is here.___

2nd time (from p. 185)

S. si - lent night.
A. Ah   Ah   si - lent night.
T. Christ the in - car - nate God.   si - lent night.
B. ___ Ah___ Ah   ho - ly night,   si - lent night.

41. THE INFANT KING

Words by
S. BARING-GOULD

Basque Noël
arranged by **DAVID WILLCOCKS**

Melody and words from *The University Carol Book*, reprinted by permission of H. Freeman & Co.

© Oxford University Press 1970

42. THERE IS NO ROSE

Anonymous, *c.* 1420
transcribed and edited by JOHN STEVENS

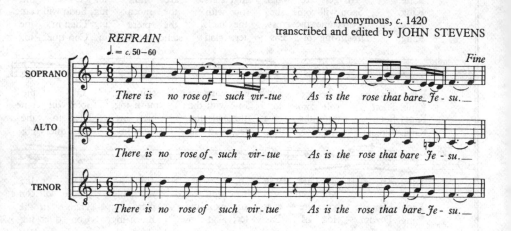

Note by John Stevens:

From a MS. roll of carols, copied out in the early 15th century and now in the Library of Trinity College, Cambridge; printed by kind permission. The carol begins and ends with the refrain (the alto part is editorial and may be omitted at will); the verses are for soloists. Small accidentals in the refrain are absent from the MS. and may be ignored if desired. The tenor has the tune throughout, and the other voices should be subordinate. The music was intended to be sung unaccompanied.

© Stainer & Bell Ltd. 1963. Reprinted by kind permission.

43. GABRIEL'S MESSAGE

Words by
S. BARING-GOULD

Basque carol
arranged by DAVID WILLCOCKS

Melody and words from *The University Carol Book*, reprinted by permission of H. Freeman & Co.

© Oxford University Press 1970

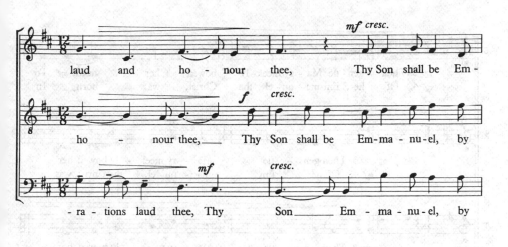

G

44. THE HOLLY AND THE IVY

English traditional carol
arranged by H. WALFORD DAVIES

Reprinted by permission of the Trustees of the late Sir Walford Davies

Also available separately (from Novello & Co., Ltd.)

© H. Walford Davies 1913

45. THE LORD AT FIRST DID ADAM MAKE

English traditional carol
arranged by DAVID WILLCOCKS

Andante (♩ = 66)

1. The Lord at first did_ A-dam make Out of the dust and clay,
And in his nos-trils breath-ed life E'en as the scrip-tures say.

And then in E-den's pa-ra-dise He pla-ced him to dwell, That

he with-in it_ should re-main, To dress and keep it well:

Now_ let good Chris-tians all be-gin An ho-ly life_ to live,_ And_

to re-joice and_ mer-ry be, For this_ is_ Christ-mas Eve.

2. And thus with-in the_ gar-den he Was set there-in to stay;
And in com-mand-ment un-to him These words the Lord did say:

ORGAN Ch. Flutes

Also available separately (X198)

© Oxford University Press 1970

TENORS and BASSES

'The fruit which in the _ gar - den grows To thee shall be for meat, Ex -

- cept the tree in the midst there - of, Of which thou shalt not eat:'

Sw. diap.

(Ped. optional)

TENORS

Ah _____ Ah _____

BARITONES

Now let good Chris - tians all be - gin An ho - ly life to live, And

BASSES

(Organ tacet) Ah _____ Ah _____

to re - joice and _ mer - ry be, For this is Christ - mas Eve.

TENORS and BASSES

3. 'For_ in the day thou shalt it touch Or dost to it come nigh,
   If_ so thou do but_ eat there-of Then thou shalt sure - ly die.'

SOPRANOS

But A - dam he did_ take no heed Un - to that on - ly thing, But

did trans - gress God's ho - ly law, And so was wrapt in sin:

SOPRANOS

Now let good Chris - tians all be - gin An ho - ly life to live, And

ALTOS

(Organ tacet)   Ah_____   Ah____

to re - joice and_ mer - ry be, For this is Christ - mas Eve.

CHOIR I — ALL VOICES

4. Now mark the good-ness of the Lord, Which he for man-kind bore;
His mer - cy soon he did ex-tend, Lost man for to re - store;

CHOIR II and ORGAN

S.
A. Ah
T.
B.

mf And then, for to re - deem our souls From death and hell - ish thrall, He
f Now let good Chris-tians all be - gin An ho - ly life to live, And

1st time: mf
2nd time: f

Ah

Ah

Ah

1st time: mf (Organ tacet)
2nd time: f

2nd time: rall. e cresc.

said his own dear Son should be The Sa - viour of us all:
to re - joice and mer - ry be, For this is Christ - mas Eve.

2nd time: rall. e cresc.

Ah
Ah

Ah

Ah

Ah

46. THE TRUTH FROM ABOVE

English traditional carol
arranged by R. VAUGHAN WILLIAMS

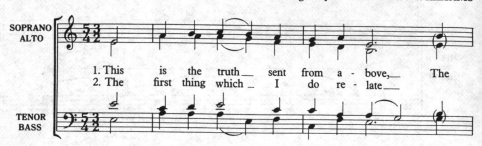

1. This is the truth sent from a bove, The
2. The first thing which I do re late

truth of God, the God of love, There-fore don't turn me
Is that God did man cre-ate; The next thing which to

from your door, But heark-en all both rich and poor.
you I'll tell Wo-man was made with man to dwell.

3. Thus we were heirs to endless woes,
Till God the Lord did interpose;
And so a promise soon did run
That he would redeem us by his Son.

4. And at that season of the year
Our blest Redeemer did appear;
He here did live, and here did preach,
And many thousands he did teach.

5. Thus he in love to us behaved,
To show us how we must be saved;
And if you want to know the way,
Be pleased to hear what he did say.

Reprinted from *Eight Traditional English Carols* (R. Vaughan Williams) by permission of Stainer & Bell Ltd.

47. TOMORROW SHALL BE MY DANCING DAY

English traditional carol
arranged by DAVID WILLCOCKS

Also available separately (X141)

© Oxford University Press 1966

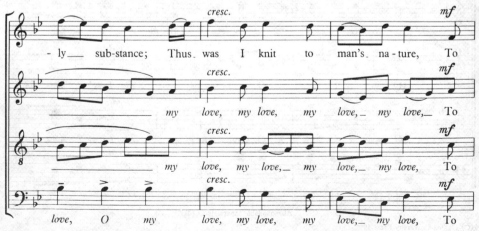

call my true_ love to_ my dance: *Sing O my_ love,*

_ *O__ my love, my love. Ah*

This have I done_ for

This have I done for

This have I done_ for

O__ my love, my love, my love; This have I done_ for

This have I done for

SOLO or SEMI-CHORUS

my___ true love.   To -

pp leggiero

my___ true love.   Sing   O   my   love,   sing___   O   my

pp leggiero

my___ true love.   Sing   O   my   love,   sing___   O   my

my___ true love.

my   true love.

S.
- mor - row shall be___ my   dan - cing day   I   would___ my true - love

A.
love.

T.
love.

B.

SOPRANO

did___ so chance   To___ see the le - gend of___ my play,   To

48. WHILE SHEPHERDS WATCHED THEIR FLOCK

Words by
NAHUM TATE (1652–1715)

Este's Psalter, 1592
Descant and organ part by DAVID WILLCOCK

1. While shep - herds watched their flocks by night, All seat - ed on the ground, The an - gel of the Lord came down, And glo - ry shone a - round.

2. 'Fear not,' said he (for might - y dread Had seized their troub - led mind); 'Glad ti - dings of great joy I bring To you and all man - kind.

3. 'To you in David's town this day
Is born of David's line
A Saviour, who is Christ the Lord;
And this shall be the sign:

4. 'The heavenly Babe you there shall find
To human view displayed,
All meanly wrapped in swathing bands,
And in a manger laid.'

5. Thus spake the Seraph; and forthwith
Appeared a shining throng
Of angels praising God, who thus
Addressed their joyful song:

Also available separately (*Six Christmas Hymns* arr. David Willcocks)

© Oxford University Press 1970

49. PATAPAN

Words by
LA MONNOYE
tr. PERCY DEARMER

Burgundian tune
arranged by REGINALD JACQUES

1. Wil - lie, take your lit - tle drum, With your whis - tle, Rob - in, come! When we hear the fife and drum,
2. Thus the men of old - en days Loved the King of kings to praise: When they hear the fife and drum,
3. God and man are now be - come More at one than fife and drum. When you hear the fife and drum,

Tu - re - lu - re -

Melody and words from *The Oxford Book of Carols*
Also available separately (T86)

© Oxford University Press 1966

*Piano plays small notes when no flute etc. available

50. ZION HEARS THE WATCHMEN'S VOICES

P. NICOLAI (1556—1608)
English words by JOHN RUTTER

J. S. BACH
(from Cantata 140)
edited by JOHN RUTTER

Small notes, crossed slurs, and bracketed dynamics and ornaments are editorial. A few discrepancies of figuring and ornamentation in the repeated section have been eliminated. Where the accompaniment is played on the organ, the melody should be picked out on a separate manual and small notes transposed up an octave where appropriate (a fully-realised continuo part is available with the orchestral hire material). Bass part has been transposed down an octave in the two sections marked ⌐___⌐. The closing chorale may effectively follow straight on from this movement.

Also available separately (X212)

© Oxford University Press 1970

20(41)

1st time

She ea - ger wakes to___ greet the day.
sie wa - chet und steht___ ei - lend auf.
Her day - star
ihr Licht wird

23

2nd time

dawns with ___ bright-est ray.
hell, ihr___ Stern geht auf.

44

47

We fol - low
Wir fol - gen

there
all

Thy feast to share,
zum Freu - den - saal

And taste the joys be - yond_ com -
Und hal - ten mit das A - bend -

50a. CHORALE

ev - 'ry__ tongue in praise u - nite.
Har - fen__ und__ mit Zim - beln schon.

an - gels__ round thy throne of light.
En - gel__ hoch__ um dei - nen Thron.

No mor - tal
Kein Aug__ hat

joy__ can__ e'er with__ heav'n's true bliss__ com - pare;
je__ ge - spürt, Kein__ Ohr__ hat je__ ge - hört

Al - le - lu - ia! Re - joice be - low, i -
Sol - che Freu - de. Des sind__ wir__ froh, i -

-o, i - o! Sing out__ in__ dul - ci ju - bi - lo.
-o, i - o! E - wig__ in__ dul - ci ju - bi - lo.

App. 1. HARK! THE HERALD ANGELS SING

Words by C. WESLEY,
T. WHITEFIELD, M. MADAN
and others

MENDELSSOHN,
adapted by W. H. CUMMINGS

1. Hark! the he-rald an-gels sing _ Glo-ry to the new-born King;
2. Christ, by high-est heav'n a-dored,_ Christ, the ev-er - last-ing Lord,
3. Hail the heav'n-born Prince of Peace! _ Hail the Sun of Right-eous-ness!

Peace on earth and mer-cy mild,_ God and sin-ners re-con-ciled:
Late in time be-hold him come_ Off-spring of a vir-gin's womb:
Light and life to all he brings,_ Ris'n with heal-ing in his wings;

Joy-ful all ye na-tions rise, _ Join the tri-umph of the skies,_
Veiled in flesh the God-head see,_ Hail th'in-car-nate De-i-ty!_
Mild he lays his glo-ry by,_ Born that man no more may die,_

With th'an-ge-lic host pro-claim, Christ is _ born in Beth-le-hem.
Pleased as man with man to dwell, Je - sus,_ our Em-ma-nu-el.
Born to raise the sons of earth, Born to_ give them se-cond birth.

UNISON

Org.

Hark! the he-rald an-gels sing Glo-ry_ to the new-born King.

Org. ped.

Reprinted by permission of Novello & Co., Ltd. For version with descant by
David Willcocks, see *Carols for Choirs 1*.

Deity pronounced Dee-ity

App. 2. O COME, ALL YE FAITHFUL

(Adeste fideles)

Words by J. F. WADE
tr. F. OAKELEY, W. T. BROOKE
and others

Melody by
J. F. WADE (c. 1711–1786)

1. O come, all ye faith - ful, Joy - ful and tri -
2. God of God, Light of
3. See how the shep - herds, Sum - moned to his
4. Sing, choirs of an - gels, Sing in ex - ul -

- um - phant, O come ye, O come ye to Beth - le - hem;
Light, Lo! he ab - hors not the Vir - gin's womb;
cra - dle, Leav - ing their flocks, draw nigh with low - ly fear;
- ta - tion, Sing, all ye cit - i - zens of heav'n a - bove;

Come and be - hold him Born the King of An - gels:
Ve - ry God, Be - got - ten, not cre - a - ted:
We too will thi - ther Bend our joy - ful foot - steps:
Glo - ry to God In the high - est:

O come, let us a - dore him, O come, let us a - dore him, O

come, let us a - dore him, Christ the Lord!

Harmony from *The English Hymnal*
For extended version arranged by David Willcocks, see *Carols for Choirs 1.*

AN ADVENT CAROL SERVICE

❡ *The Congregation shall stand while the Choir sings the* Matin Responsory *at the West End of the Church, followed by the hymn* Come, thou Redeemer of the earth *in procession to the Choir stalls.*

❡ *All shall then be bidden to prayer in these words:*

BELOVED in Christ, as we await the great festival of Christmas let us prepare ourselves so that we may be shown its true meaning. Let us hear, in lessons from Holy Scripture, how the prophets of Israel foretold that God would visit and redeem his waiting people. Let us rejoice, in our carols and hymns, that the good purpose of God is being mightily fulfilled. Let us celebrate the promise that our Lord and Saviour, Jesus Christ, will bring all men and all things into the glory of God's eternal kingdom. The blind receive their sight, and the lame walk, the lepers are cleansed, and the deaf hear, the dead are raised up, and the poor have the Gospel preached to them.

But first, let us pray for the world which God so loves, for those who have not heard the good news of God, or who do not believe it; for those who walk in darkness and the shadow of death; and for the Church in this place and everywhere, that it may be freed from all evil and fear, and may in pure joy lift up the light of the love of God.

These prayers and praises let us humbly offer to God, in the words which Christ himself taught us:

Our Father, which [who] art in heaven, hallowed be thy name; thy kingdom come; thy will be done; in [on] earth as it is in heaven. Give us this day our daily bread. And forgive us our trespasses, as we forgive them that [those who] trespass against us. And lead us not into temptation; But deliver us from evil. For thine is the kingdom, the power, and the glory, for ever and ever. Amen.

❡ *Then shall the Congregation sit.*
[*The Readers of the Lessons should be appointed after a definite order; in a Cathedral, for instance, from a Chorister up to a Bishop.*
Each Reader should proceed to the Reading Desk at the beginning of the last verse of the preceding carol or hymn; and announce his Lesson by the descriptive sentence attached to it. At the end of the Lesson, the Reader should pause and say: Thanks be to God.]

FIRST LESSON
The Prophet proclaims good news to a people in exile.   ISAIAH XL, 1–8

SECOND LESSON
The Lord promises to send his people a righteous King.   JEREMIAH XXIII, 5–6

THIRD LESSON
The Lord promises that the King will come to Israel in peace.   ZECHARIAH IX, 9–10

FOURTH LESSON
The Prophet foretells the advent of the desire of all nations.   HAGGAI II, 6–9

FIFTH LESSON
The Prophet foretells the glory of the kingdom of God.   ISAIAH XXXV, 1–6

SIXTH LESSON
The angel Gabriel salutes the Blessed Virgin Mary.   ST LUKE I, 26–35, 38

ALTERNATIVE SIXTH LESSON
St Paul declares the good purpose of God.   ROMANS VIII, 28–39

℣   *The Congregation shall stand for the seventh lesson.*

SEVENTH LESSON
Jesus proclaims the coming of the kingdom of God.   ST MARK I, 1–15

VESPER RESPONSORY

℣   *To be said by Priest and People, alternately*

Priest   Judah and Jerusalem, fear not, nor be dismayed;
People   Tomorrow go ye forth, and the Lord, he will be with you.
Priest   Stand ye still, and ye shall see the salvation of the Lord.
People   Tomorrow go ye forth, and the Lord, he will be with you.
Priest   Glory be to the Father, and to the Son, and to the Holy Ghost.
People   Tomorrow go ye forth, and the Lord, he will be with you.

℣   *All shall keep silence for a time.*

COLLECT

Priest   We wait for thy loving kindness, O Lord.
People   In the midst of thy temple.

Let us pray.

O God, who makest us glad with the yearly expectation of thy coming,
Grant that we, who with joy receive thy only-begotten Son as our
Redeemer, may without fear behold him when he shall come to be our
Judge, even thy Son our Lord Jesus Christ; who liveth and reigneth
with thee and the Holy Ghost, one God, world without end. *Amen.*

THE BLESSING

Go forth into the world in peace; be of good courage; hold fast that
which is good; render to no man evil for evil; strengthen the faint-hearted;
support the weak; help the afflicted; honour all men; love and serve the
Lord, rejoicing in the power of the Holy Spirit.

And the blessing of God Almighty, the Father, the Son, and the Holy
Spirit, be upon you, and remain with you for ever. *Amen.*